Cable Needle Freedom

Carole Wulster

Art Direction: Patti Pierce Stone
Editing: Dara J. Tatum

Introduction:

Until a few years ago, I never realized that cable knitting is one of the easiest of knitting techniques. I always admired any pattern that was comprised of cables, braids or multi-stitch twists. However, I seldom would tackle such a project. I knew that I had the knitting expertise, but the complexity of the chart, the constant counting, and the pesky cable needle were enough to send me looking for a different project.

Then I discovered how to cable without a cable needle. Cable knitting without a cable needle is not my invention. In fact, I am sure that those who knit the first cable patterns did not use a cable needle. On the day I determined to rid myself of the cable needle forever, I never dreamed that I would open myself to an epiphany regarding both cable knitting and knitting in general.

In learning to cable without a cable needle, I was forced to look at the fabric I was producing. I realized that within a few rows of the first cable crossings the fabric was providing visual cues as to the movement of the stitches. I no longer needed the chart. I could see whether I was supposed to move stitches to the right or the left. I was stunned. I finally saw all the connections between the symbols and the fabric. At long last, I had achieved visualization.

Now, I can barely remember the time when cables were intimidating. The technique is so simple; I often wonder why I had not explored cable knitting in this manner earlier in my knitting career.

Once the cable needle is gone, and once your eyes become your extra tool, something indescribable happens. It is almost like eye hand coordination in sports. One look at the work and your fingers know what to do. I now knit cables without step by step thought.

If you have been cable knitting for years or are venturing into cables for the first time, I know that you will master cable knitting without an extra needle quickly. As time goes on, and you reach the peak of your comfort level, you will find that you will be skipping some of the steps that are presented here and the process of turning a cable will be even more fluid.

I hope this little book will provide you with the tools you need to knit the most intricate of cables with speed, pleasure and pride.

Carole

Contents

* Sweater patterns are written for pullover and cardigan.

Cable Knitting

Cables and twisted stitches are implemented by crossing one set of stitches over another. Traditionally, to implement the cross of several stitches over another set of stitches, a tool named a cable needle is used. The cable needle can be any double pointed instrument that allows the knitter to slip a prescribed number of stitches off the non working needle and hold those stitches to the front or the back of the work. This allows the knitter to work the next set of stitches from the left needle before working the stitches from the cable needle. The cable needle allows the knitter to change the sequence in which a certain number of stitches are worked, thereby crossing stitches over one another. The cable needle is usually 3 – 5" long. In some cases there is a curve in the cable needle to prevent the stitches from slipping off either end.

The cable needle serves a useful function, but interferes with both the flow of the work and with the ability to visualize the cable or crossed stitch in progress.

With a little practice, cabling and twisted stitches can be implemented without a cable needle.

The benefits of learning to cable knit without a cable needle are:
- Flow to the knitting
- Visualization of the cable in progress
- One less tool

2

Chart Fundamentals

Before we can begin to knit, it is important to learn how to read a cable chart. The cable chart is the map to building the textured stitch in the actual knitted fabric.

Charts can be very intimidating with the various symbols. If you find that you are symbol challenged, let us attempt clear that up once and for all. The symbols in charts instruct the knitter on how to implement each stitch to create a fabric.

For clarity, it is important to find a vocabulary for describing the knitted fabric and chart reading.

Knitted Fabric

The public face of the fabric is the side of the fabric that is meant to be seen. In this book, the public face is named the right side or RS. The side of the fabric that is meant to be unseen is referred to as the wrong side or WS.

Chart Reading

Flat knitting is the term for knitting with two needles and working in rows. All stitches on the left needle are worked. This is considered Row 1 and the right side of the fabric. After the last stitch is worked, the piece is turned and all stitches are worked again, Row 2 and the wrong side of the fabric. In stockinette stitch Row 1 (RS) all stitches are knit. Row 2 (WS) all stitches are purled. To read a chart for flat knitting, Row 1 is the first RS row and is read from right to left. Row 2 is the first WS row and is read from left to right.

In flat knitting, the norm is that all odd numbered rows are RS rows (public face rows) and are read from right to left. All even rows are WS rows (inside of the fabric) and are read from left to right.

The chart always represents the right side of the fabric. If you are looking at a color chart, your eyes will pull the pattern out instantly, however you might find symbols defeat your ability to see the pattern.

We are going to start with the most basic symbols, the knit and the purl stitch. There is actually a relationship between the look of the symbol and the look of the finished stitch.

When we are first taught to knit, we are taught how to differentiate between the knit stitch and the purl stitch on the fabric. The knit stitch is a flat vertical stitch in the fabric. It almost looks like an elongated heart. The signature of the purl stitch is the horizontal bump it produces in the fabric. In the symbol lexicon, the knit stitch is represented by a vertical line and purl stitch is represented by a horizontal line.

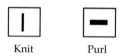

Knit   Purl

As our understanding progresses, we realize that working a knit stitch on the right side of the fabric produces a purl stitch on the wrong side. The same holds true for the purl stitch. A purled stitch on the right side produces a knit stitch on the wrong side.

Since a chart represents the right side of the fabric and the right side only, some symbols need to reflect how the stitch is worked on both sides to produce the right side effect; therefore the vertical line and the horizontal line have a double meaning. Each has a right side fabric meaning and a wrong side fabric meaning.

Knit on the right side, purl on the wrong side.

Purl on the right side, knit on the wrong side

A knit 2, purl 2 rib would be represented on a chart as:

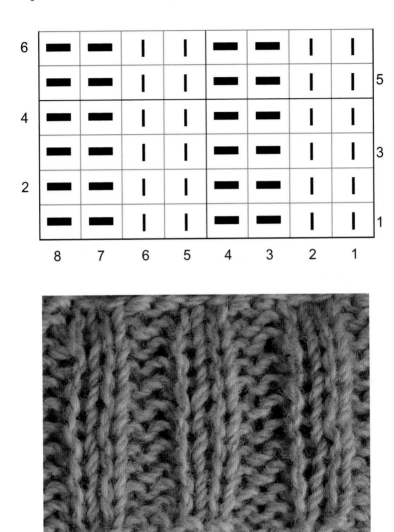

In flat knitting, the chart is read from right to left for right side of the fabric. Read left to right for the wrong side of the fabric. Therefore this chart would be read as
Row 1:
RS (right side: read from right to left) K2, P2, K2, P2
Row 2:
WS (wrong side: read from left to right). K2, P2, K2, P2

Look closely at the picture of the swatch. Compare the swatch to the chart. Do you see the vertical lines of knit stitches and the vertical lines of the purl stitches in the swatch? Look again at the chart. In your mind, place the chart stitches over the swatch stitches. Allow yourself to visualize the chart as worked stitch. See the correlation between the symbol and the actual stitch.

Reading Cable Symbols

In a text description, cables are often named by the direction in which the stitches cross one another. For example, you may see written cable directions written out as RC Rope. This is translated as Right Cross Rope Cable. Row by row instructions would be provided for working one vertical repeat of the cable. Reading the instructions while knitting does not permit the knitter to visualize what is actually happening with the cable. A chart with cable symbols allows the knitter to see the cable cross before working the stitches.

Cable symbols provide the following information in graphic form:
1. the number of stitches in the cable
2. the direction in which the stitches will cross over to create the cable
3. the manner in which the stitches will be worked once the stitches are crossed.

8

The symbol spans the number of stitches worked in the cable. If the total number of stitches in a cable is four, then four stitches are blocked out on the chart. A diagonal line in the symbol represents the direction in which the stitches will cross over each other.

This is the symbol for a 4 stitch cable in which two stitches cross from left to right. The cross is represented by the diagonal line moving from bottom left to upper right. In other words, the diagonal line points to the right. This is described as a right cross.

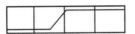

This symbol represents a 4 stitch cable in which two stitches cross from right to left. The cross is represented by the diagonal line moving from bottom right to upper left. The diagonal line points to the left. This crossing is described as a left cross.

When using a cable needle, to cross to the right as shown in the first symbol, the first two stitches are slipped to the cable needle and held to the back, the next two stitches are worked. The final step is to work the stitches from the cable needle.

To cross to the left, as shown in the second symbol, the first two stitches are slipped to a cable needle and held to the front, the next two stitches are worked. The two stitches from the cable needle are then worked. The above symbols do not describe how to work the stitches in the cable. To represent the stitches, add the stitch symbols for the knit stitch.

The knit symbol added to the cable symbol provides information on how to work the stitches.

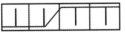

Cable needle instructions would read: Slip two sts to cable needle, hold in back of work. Knit the next 2 stitches on the left needle. K 2 from cable needle. This maneuver creates a right cross.

Traditional instructions would read: Slip two sts to cable needle, hold in front of the work. Knit the next 2 stitches from the left needle. Knit 2 from cable needle. This maneuver creates a left cross.

The direction is which the cable is crossed is determined by whether the stitches on the cable needle are held to the front or to the back.

Those of you who are already adept at cable knitting are probably saying, "yes, but I already know this". For those of you new to cable knitting, you may feel a bit lost. Since the whole point of this book is not using a cable needle, the most important information in the above description for our purposes is the diagonal line. **The diagonal line is the visual cue for the direction in which the stitches will cross.**

It is very important to try to visualize this from the chart. The number of grid squares represents the number of stitches in the cable, the diagonal line represents the direction of cable crossing, the stitch symbols represent how the stitches are to be worked.

Below, and on the adjacent page, are two rope cables. Each cable is 6 stitches, one cable crosses to the right, the other to the left, and each cable is worked over knit stitches.

10

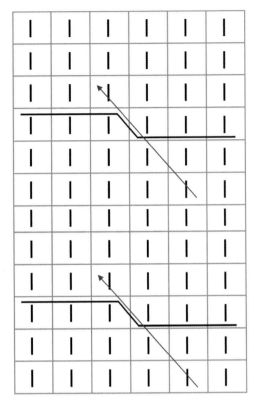

The last piece of information that the cable chart provides is how to work the individual stitches once they are crossed. Compare the arrows on the chart to the arrows on the fabric.

Summary

The cable symbol provides us with the following information to be read in the following sequence:

1. Total number of stitches in the cable.
2. Number of stitches to cross.
3. The direction in which the stitches will cross
4. Stitch symbols directing the way in which each stitch is to be worked after the cross.

Read this cable symbol as:

1. Total number of stitches = 4
2. Number of stitches to cross: 2 over 2
3. Cable Direction = to the right (diagonal line points to the right).
4. Stitch symbol directions = K4

Read this cable symbol as:

1. Total number of stitches = 4
2. Number of stitches to cross: 2 over 2
3. Cable Direction = to the right (diagonal line points to the right)
4. Stitch symbol directions = K2, p2.

The two cables represented above are symmetrical. There are an equal number of stitches on each side of the diagonal line.

Next are two examples of asymmetrical crossing. In first symbol below, three stitches are crossed over 1. Three stitches move to the right. In the second, three stitches are again crossed over 1, but the stitches move to the left.

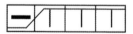

Read this cable symbol as:

1. Number of stitches = 4
2. Number of stitches to cross: 3 over 1
3. Cable Direction = to the right (diagonal line points to the right)
4. Stitch symbol directions = K3, p1.

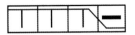

Read this cable symbol as:

5. Number of stitches = 4
6. Number of stitches to cross: 3 over 1
7. Cable Direction = to the left (diagonal line points to the left)
8. Stitch symbol directions = P1, k3.

Once you have accustomed your eye to identify the direction of the diagonal line, you are half way there. At this moment you may still be thinking 'diagonal line points to the right' or 'diagonal line points to the left' but soon, your eyes and hands will coordinate. You will not be thinking right or left. Your hands will just know which way to move the stitches just as you know in which direction to turn the wheel of car to turn right our left.

3

Cabling Without a Cable Needle

Once the knitter grasps the concept that the cable or twisted stitch can only go in one of two directions, it is much easier to understand the benefits of cabling without a needle. Cable knitting is very visual. As you knit you need to observe the progress of the work. By removing the cable needle, the knitter can always see in which direction the stitches are being crossed. Both hands and eye will know if a error is being made. In addition to the benefits of visualization, the speed at which the cables will be built without the cable needle is a wonder.

The only way to learn the technique is to actually do it. Below you will find three exercises. The first two are just to get the feel of crossing stitches without a cable needle. In the first exercise, you will cross 2 stitches over 2 stitches. The second exercise is crossing 3 stitches over 3 stitches. The third may make you wary because the chart looks complex to begin with, but by the time you finish it, not only will you have completed 2/3 of a gorgeous hat, but you will be a master of cable knitting without a cable needle.

The most important tool in cabling without a cable needle is your needles. To make life easier, choose a set of needles that
  1. have a defined point
  2. are smooth but not slippery (bamboo, wood, coated aluminum or casein, not smooth metal).

In the exercises I have used a worsted weight, 100% wool yarn and a US size 8 or 9 (5 or 5.5 mm needle).

Let's get started!

Exercise 1

Legend

| Knit on the RS, Purl on WS

— Purl on RS, Knit on WS

Left 4 St Rope Cable

Right 4 St Rope Cable

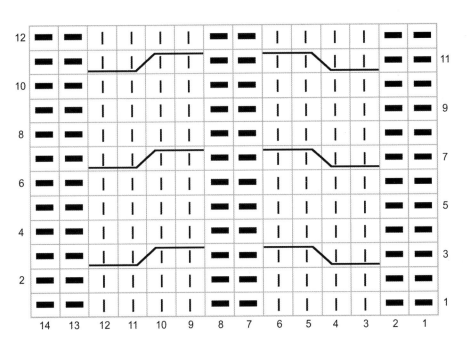

Cast on 14 stitches:

Row 1 (RS):* p2, k 4, repeat from * end 2.
Row 2 (WS): K the k sts, p the p sts.

Note Row 3 is the first cable row.
We are going to do two 4 st cables. The first crosses to the left and the second crosses to the right.

Purl the first 2 stitches.

Look at the needle. The next 4 stitches are knit stitches. We know from our cable symbol that the first cable is worked over 4 stitches. The diagonal line in the first cable symbol points to the left so it is a left crossing cable. There are two stitches on each side of the diagonal line; therefore we will have a 2 over 2 cross.

To cross the stitches:

1. Insert right needle tip into the back of stitches 3 & 4.

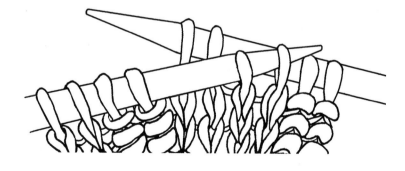

2. Slide stitches onto right needle. Stitches 1 & 2 will drop to front.

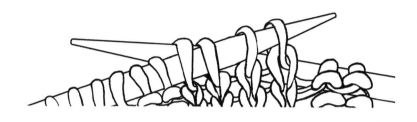

3. Pick up dropped stitches (1 & 2) with left needle point as illustrated.

16

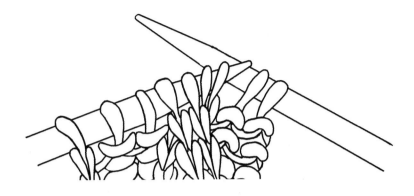

4. Slip first two stitches from the right needle point to left needle point.

5. Knit the 4 stitches.

Stop. Look at your work. Note that two stitches are crossed to the left.

Purl 2 stitches.

Work right cross over next 4 sts.

To implement this right cross without a cable needle:

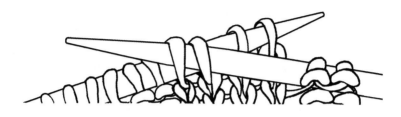

1. Insert right needle tip into the front of stitches 3 & 4.

2. Slide stitches onto right needle. Stitches 1 & 2 will drop to the back.

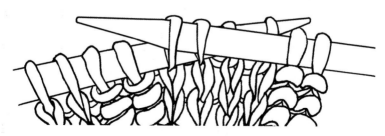

3. Pick up dropped stitches (1 & 2) with the left needle point.

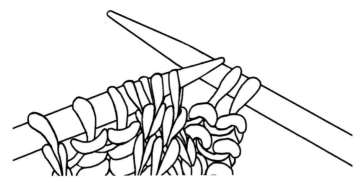

4. Slip first two stitches from the right needle point to left needle point.

5. Knit the 4 stitches.

Please Note: The crossing is set up before you work the first stitch. This will always give you a visual check to insure the cross is going in the correct direction.
End Purl 2.

Stop and take a deep breath. I know that tension fills the knitter's soul as soon as stitches are off the needle almost floating in air so to speak. If you are terribly uncomfortable with the feeling, here is a tip:
Left Cross: Stitches slipped off the left needle are in the front. When sliding the stitches off the needle use the thumb of the right hand to support them until the left needle tip is inserted.
Right Cross: Stitches slipped off the left needle are in the back. When sliding the stitches off the needle use the index finger of the right hand to support them until the left needle tip has been fully inserted.

Back to knitting! Work three rows even. According to the chart, knit the knit stitches and purl the purl stitches on rows 4, 5, and 6. Work cables on row 7. Work 8, 9, & 10 even. Work cables on row 11. Work row 12. Bind off.

Exercise 2

Legend

| | Knit on the RS, Purl on WS

| - | Purl on RS, Knit on WS

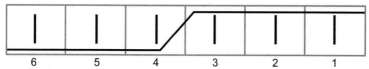

6 St Left Cable Cross

Insert right needle point into the back of the 4th, 5th & 6th stitch on the left needle. Slide stitches onto right needle. Stitches 1, 2 & 3 will drop to front. Pick up dropped stitches with left needle point. Slip first three stitches from right needle to left needle. Knit 6 stitches.

6 st Right Cable Cross

Insert right needle point into the front of the 4th, 5th & 6th stitch on the left needle. Slide stitches onto right needle. Stitches 1, 2 & 3 will drop to back. Pick up dropped stitches with left needle point. Slip first three stitches from right needle to left needle. Knit 6 stitches.

6 St Ropes

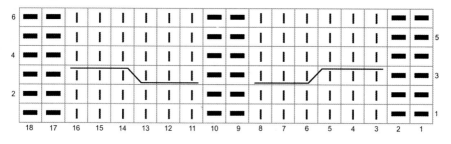

Cast on 18 stitches. Work 6 rows of chart 2 times. Bind off.

This may have been slightly more difficult than the 2 over 2 cross, however with practice it will become second nature.

At this point, I need to make a confession. I really fail at practice, practice, practice on a swatch. I can rarely discipline myself to practice a new technique on a non-project. I think that is why the two exercises above produce such small swatches. In spite of the size of both swatches they hold a wealth of information for future cable knitting.

Before continuing into the next exercise which will produce a wearable garment, let's pause a minute and look at what we have learned so far.

Once you have done one cable crossing, the chart is no longer needed. When the cable row is reached, the direction of the cross is evident by the one below it.

When the right needle point is inserted in the front of stitches on the left needle, the cross will be to the right. When right needle point is inserted in the back of stitches on the left needle, the cross will be to the left. Therefore:

- Front Insertion = right cross
- Back Insertion = left cross
   o Front = Right
   o Back = Left

The index finger on the right hand is used to support the stitches in a right cross, the thumb is used to support the stitches in left cross.

Once you have practiced the cable crossings enough, you will be able to look at a chart and look at the diagonal lines. If the line points to the right, your fingers will automatically insert the needle into the front and if the line points to the left, then your needle will move to the back. It will become as much a part of you as inserting the needle to knit or purl. You don't think about the way in which you insert the needle for the knit stitch, you just do it.

The swatches also provide more information.

1. Cables are crossed on the right side of the fabric.
2. It is easier to do cables in the flat than in the round as it is easier to count right side rows in the flat than in the round.
3. Knitting and purling are used in each row; therefore there really is no single advantage to knitting in the round other than seaming.
4. At the cable crossing, the fabric width is decreased by half the width the same number of stitches would produce in stockinette.
5. The fabric weight is doubled at the cable crossings.

21

This information answers many questions for knitters regarding patterns with cables or crossed stitches. In many of these patterns, the designer gives the gauge in the border stitch or stockinette stitch. The reason for this is that each different cable produces a different gauge. The designer works out all the gauges and the number of stitches need to produce the finished size. However, to save the knitter time and yarn, the designer assumes that if the knitter can reproduce the same gauge created in the border or stockinette stitch, then the cable gauges will work out to be the same.

Most Aran patterns are written for flat knitting (two needles) with seams. Seaming is very easy using the mattress stitch on cabled sweaters. Many knitters do not count rows but measure. When knitting in the flat, this can create a problem in seaming as gauge may have changed and there may be more rows in one piece than another. However, with vertical cable panels, the knitter counts the numbers of cable crossings or vertical repeats of the pattern. If no errors are made, there will be the same number of rows in pieces that need to be matched, thus easy seaming.

Exercise 3

Exercise 3 is a real project, not just an exercise. When you are finished, the result will be a lovely hat and you will be an expert at cable knitting without a needle.

Please don't be intimidated by the chart. It is a simple braid pattern bordered on each edge by garter stitch. Keep in mind that the stitch crossings are only worked on right side rows. I love braids or plait patterns. As you are working, you will see the knit stitches of the braid form curved lines. Wonderful!

This hat is pattern is very versatile. Once you have mastered cable knitting, you can replace the band design with any cable combination that will yield approximately 5" in width. It is also a great pattern for yarn remainders.

The band of the cap is knit in one long piece, 5 vertical repeats of the chart. The band is then sewn together to form a circle. The crown of the hat is then picked up from one edge of the band and knit in the round. Since the public face of the crown is reverse stockinette stitch (purl), you will use a YO (yarn over) to turn the hat inside out. This will enable you to work on the wrong side and use the knit stitch until the hat is completed. Pay careful attention to the details of the instructions. I will work along with you for the first few rows.

Materials:
250 yds of worsted weight wool
Sample:
Black Water Abbey Worsted Weight Color: Butter

8 markers
Needles:
Size 9 (5.5 mm) for the band.
Size 8 (5 mm) 16" circular and set of 5 dpns for the crown.

| Knit on the RS, Purl on WS

— Purl on RS, Knit on WS

Left Cable Cross (Knit)

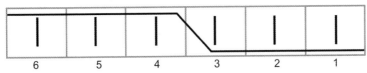

Insert right needle point into the **back** of the 4th, 5th & 6th stitch on the left needle. Slide stitches onto right needle. Stitches 1, 2 & 3 will drop to front. Pick up dropped stitches with left needle point. Slip first three stitches from right needle to left needle. Knit 6 stitches.

Right Cable Cross (Knit)

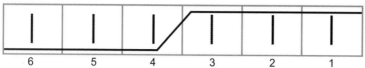

Insert right needle point into the **front** of the 4th, 5th & 6th stitch on the left needle. Slide stitches onto right needle. Stitches 1, 2 & 3 will drop to back. Pick up dropped stitches with left needle point. Slip first three stitches from right needle to left needle. Knit 6 stitches.

Right Cross with Purl

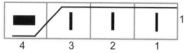

Insert right needle point into the **front** of the 2nd, 3rd, & 4th stitch on the left needle. Slide stitches onto right needle. Stitch 1 will drop to the back. Pick up dropped stitch with left needle point. Slip first three stitches from right needle to left needle. K3, p1.

Left Cross with Purl

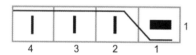

Insert right needle point into the **back** of the 4th stitch on the left needle. Slide stitch onto right needle. Stitch 1, 2, and 3 will drop to the front. Pick up dropped stitches with left needle point. Slip first stitch from right needle to left needle. P1, k3

Let's work the beginning of the hat together.
Cast on 38 sts.
Work a set-up row. The set-up row is the wrong side.

Set-up Row: K2 (2st garter border) place marker, *k4, p6 repeat from * 3 times total. End k4, place maker, k2 (2st garter stitch border).

Note: The 2 stitches on either end are border stitches worked in garter stitch. In other words, on every row the first two stitches and the last two stitches are worked in the knit stitch whether you are on the right side or the wrong side.

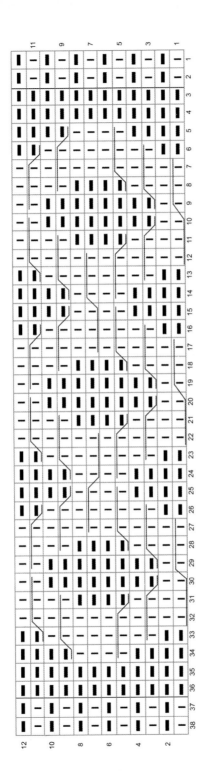

25

Row 1: From the chart K2, pass marker, *p4, work right cable cross, repeat from * 3 times, end p4, pass marker, k2.
Row 2: K2, pass marker, *k4, p6. Repeat from * 3 times. End k4, pass marker, K2.

On row 3, we are going to see the logic of the symbols and the stitch movement. K2, pass marker, p3. Stop. Look at the next 4 stitches on the left needle. The first stitch is a purl stitch; the next 3 are knit stitches. Now look at the chart. On the row below, Row 2. Note the first group of purl stitches (4 stitches). On row 3, the current working row on the needle, the 4th purl stitch needs to be moved from its current location to stitch place 9. To accomplish this, cross 3 knit stitches over 1 purl stitch. The diagonal line in the symbol tells us that the three knit stitches are going to move to the right and one purl stitch will move to the left.

Insert the right needle point into the front of stitches 2, 3, & 4 on the left needle. Slide the stitches off the left needle, stitch 1, a purl stitch, will drop to the back. Pick up stitch 1 with the left needle point. Using the left needle point slip the first 3 stitches from the right needle back to the left needle. Now the purl stitch is in position 4. K3, p1.

The next 4 stitches on the left needle are 3 knits 1 purl. The purl stitch needs to be moved to position 1. The diagonal line points to the left, therefore three knit stitches will be crossed over the one purl stitch to the left. Insert the right needle point through the back of the 4th stitch on the left needle, a purl stitch. Slide the stitch onto the right needle, the first 3 knit sts will fall to the front. Pick up the purl stitch with the left needle and slip the first stitch from the right needle to the left needle. P1, k3.

This is as hard as it gets. The important thing to note is that you can see the logical stitch placement.

Continue working the chart.

When you have completed the chart, repeat chart 4 more times. You will have worked the braid a total of 5 times. The piece will measure between 19 – 21"

Bind off.

Seam edge to edge with mattress stitch matching the braid.

With 16" circular needle, pick up 104 sts along the edge (approx 4 sts for every 5 rws.). Place marker, join. Purl one round.

The public face of the crown is reverse stockinette (all purl). However, most knitters find that the glory of working in the round is that they never need purl. To accomplish this, the crown needs to be worked on the wrong side. To turn the hat inside out and knit the remainder of the crown, YO (yarn over) and **TURN**. Push the hat into the open area of your circular needle. It will be inside out.

Knit all the stitches in the round until you get to the last stitch before the marker. Knit the last stitch together with the YO. This action will take care of any hole. Continue to knit all rounds following the directions below:

On the next rnd, *knit 13, place marker. Repeat from * to end. You will have 8 markers total. Please be sure to mark the beginning of the round marker with by tying a piece of yarn on it.

Decrease Rnd: K2tog, *knit to two sts before marker, SSK, pass marker, K2tog. Repeat from * to last two sts of rnd. SSK. (11 sts between markers)

Continue as follows:

Work 3 rnds in stockinette.
Work 1 decrease rnd.
Stop at the end of the decrease rnd when there are 5 sts between markers. 40 sts total.
Arrange your stitches on 4 double point needles. There will be 10 stitches on each needle with a marker in the middle of each needle.
Work 3 rnds in stockinette.
On the next rnd:
Needle 1: K2tog, K1, SSK, pass marker, k2tog, K1, SSK
Repeat on each needle.
24 stitches remaining.
On the next rnd, k2tog. 12 stitches remaining.
Cut the yarn leaving an 8 – 10" tail.

Thread tapestry needle. Run tapestry needle through all the stitches as if to purl starting with the first stitch on the round. Pull to close. Run the tapestry needle through again. Weave in the end.
Weave in all other ends.
Turn to the right side.
Block and shape.

Honeycomb, Honeycomb

The honeycomb sweater pattern uses a central panel of the honeycomb stitch bordered on either side by a simple braid and a rope cable. Please note on the chart the outermost cable (rope) on either side is turned every sixth row and the honeycomb and braids are turned every third row. Analyzing the chart before knitting begins aids in visualization.

I place markers during the setup of the pattern panels. Once I have worked row 3, I remove the markers except for the ones on either end separating the panel from the border stitches. The markers are really in the way once you begin knitting the panels. The stitches will speak to your fingers.

Pattern is pictured as a cardigan but directions for a pullover style are included.
Sizes: S (M, L)
Finished Chest: 44(48, 52)"
Materials:
Yarn:
Black Water Abbey Worsted Weight (7 ,8, 9).
Color: Wine
Needles: Sizes: 7, 9
Accessories: Tapestry needle, markers.
Buttons: 8 7/8" buttons

Gauge: 4 sts = 1" 6 rws = 1" over Border Stitch when blocked. Knit a swatch in the border stitch. Block it and then measure.

Note: The symbol for the k on the right side, purl on the wrong side is a blank stitch in this chart. It makes the chart easier to read.

Border Stitch:
Row 1: (Right Side) *K1, p1. repeat from *
Row 2: (Wrong Side) K across.

Knit on the right side, purl on the wrong side

Purl on the right side, knit on the wrong side

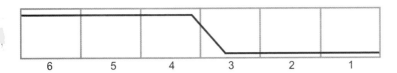

6	5	4	3	2	1

6 st Left Cross

Insert right needle point into the back of the 4th, 5th & 6th stitch on the left needle. Slide stitches onto right needle. Stitches 1, 2 & 3 will drop to front. Pick up dropped stitches with left needle point. Slip first three stitches from right needle to left needle. Knit 6 stitches.

6 st Right Cross

Insert right needle point into the front of the 4th, 5th & 6th stitch on the left needle. Slide stitches onto right needle. Stitches 1, 2 & 3 will drop to back. Pick up dropped stitches with left needle point. Slip first three stitches from right needle to left needle. Knit 6 stitches.

4 st Left Cross

Insert right needle point into the back of the 3rd & 4th stitch on the left needle. Slide stitches onto right needle. Stitches 1 & 2 will drop to front. Pick up dropped stitches with left needle point. Slip first two stitches from right needle to left needle. Knit 4 stitches.

4st Right Cross

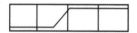

Insert right needle point into the front of the 3rd & 4th stitch on the left needle. Slide stitches onto right needle. Stitches 1 & 2 will drop to front. Pick up dropped stitches with left needle point. Slip first two stitches from right needle to left needle. Knit 4 stitches.

Place Marker
　O　place marker

Cardigan or Pullover Back:
With size 7 needle, cast on 118 (128, 138) sts. Work 4 rows of Border Stitch. Change to size 9 needle to work body.
To establish pattern:
Row 1: Work 16 (17, 18) sts in Border Stitch place marker, follow chart placing markers between each section.
When you reach the center section which is the honeycomb, repeat the pattern 4 (5, 6) times-32 (40, 48) sts, complete chart, work the last 16 (17, 18)) sts in Border Stitch. Continue working rows in Chart 1 (repeating the 8 rows) until piece measures 12.5(13.5, 13.5)" from beg. Place underarm marker. Continue in pattern until piece measures 23 (25, 25.5)" from the beginning. Bind off.

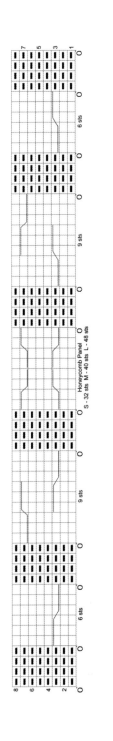

Honeycomb Panel
S - 32 sts M - 40 sts L - 48 sts

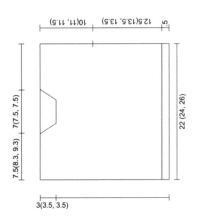

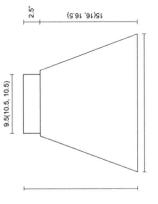

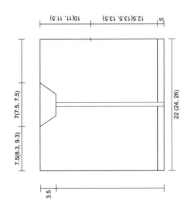

Cardigan Fronts:

Note: 2 honeycombs are worked on each front. Repeat the Honeycomb Panel twice.

The cardigan fronts are worked at the same time to limit confusion on shaping. Have two balls of yarn prepared.

Using smaller needle, with the first ball cast on 63(64, 69) stitches. Drop yarn. Using the second ball of yarn, cast on 63(64, 69) sts. Work Border stitch for 4 rows.

Change to larger needles.

Setup Row: (Row 1) Right side, work 16 (17, 18) sts in Border stitch, place marker, p 4, place marker, k 6, place marker, p4, place marker, k9, place marker, p4, place marker, k 16, place marker, p 4(8, 8). Drop yarn. Pick up yarn for second front and p4(8, 8) place marker, k 16, place marker, p 4, place marker, k 9, place marker, p4, place marker, k 6, place marker, p 4, place marker, work last 16 (17,18) sts in Border stitch.

Row 2: (Wrong Side): Work Border stitch. Follow row 2 on the chart. Work honeycomb section twice (16 purl stitches), knit 4(8,8) edge stitches. Drop yarn. Pick up yarn for second piece. Work 4(8, 8) edge stitches, follow the chart starting at the honeycomb. Repeat honeycomb stitches twice (16 purl stitches) complete chart.

Row 3: Work border pattern as established, follow Row 3 of the chart, until two sets of honeycomb stitches are completed, work edge stitches. Drop yarn. Pick up yarn for second piece, work edge stitches, work the honeycomb twice, continue with established pattern on the chart, end with Border stitch.

Work in established pattern until piece measures 12.5(13.5, 13.5)" from beg. Place underarm marker.

Continue to work until piece measures 19.5(21.5, 22)" from the beginning ending on a WS row.

Begin Neck Shaping:

RS: Work across first presenting cardigan front. Drop yarn. Pick up yarn for second front, bind off 14(11, 11) sts. Complete row.

WS: Work across first presenting cardigan front. Drop yarn. Pick up yarn for second presenting cardigan front, bind off 14(11, 11) sts. Complete Row.

Continue working pattern and at the same time decrease 1 st at each neck edge, every other row 10(9, 9) times.

When piece measures same as back, bind off 40, (44, 49) shoulder stitches.

Pullover Front:

Work as for back and at the same time when piece measures 20(21.5, 22)" from the beginning ending on wrong side row.

Neck Shaping:

Work to center 24 (26, 26) sts. Attach another ball of yarn and bind off center 24 (26, 26) sts. Complete row. Working both sides at once, dec 1 st at each neck edge, every other row 7 times.

Continue in pat st until piece measures the same as the back.

Bind off 40(44, 49) sts across each shoulder.

Seam Shoulders.

Sleeves

The sleeves are worked from the top down. Establish pattern according to instructions below and work decreases.

Beginning at armhole marker, with right side facing pick up 108 (118, 122) sts as follows:

Row1: Right Side: [Pick up 9 (8, 8) sts, skip 1] 6(4, 2) times. Pick up 0 (9, 9) sts, skip 1] 0 (3, 5) times to shoulder, pick up a stitch at the shoulder. Pick up 0 (9, 9) sts, skip 1] 0 (3, 5) times, pick up 9 (8, 8) sts, skip 1] 6(4, 2) times to underarm maker.

The pattern in the sleeve is 5 single honeycomb panels bordered by reverse stockinette stitch (purl on the right side).

Set up pattern as follows:

Set-up Row: WS: K 18(23, 25),place marker, p 8, place marker, k 8, place marker, p 8, place marker, k 8, place marker, p 8, place marker, k 8, place marker, p 6, place marker, k 8, p 8, place marker, k 18(23, 25)

Row 1: RS: P 23 (23, 25), pass marker, k8, pass marker, p8, pass marker, k8, pass marker, p 8, pass marker, k6, pass marker, p 8, pass marker, k8, pass marker, p 8 pass marker, k 8, p 18(23, 25).

Row 2: K the knit stitches purl the purl stitches.

Row 3: Purl the purl stitches, work row 3 of the honeycomb section of the chart over 8 knit stitches between each marker. Continue in this fashion working the honeycomb panels for the length of the sleeve.

When sleeve measures 1" begin decreasing:

Sleeve decreases:

S: Dec 1 st on each side of sleeve every 3 rows 28 times.

M: Dec 1 st on each side every 2 rows 3 times and then every 3 rows 28 times.

L: Dec 1 st on each side every 2 rows 9 times then every 3 rows 24 times. 50 (56, 56) sts

Continue until sleeve measures one row short of 15 (16, 16.5)" from the shoulder. On the last wrong side row decrease 3 (5, 5) sts evenly using k2 tog.

Change to size 7 needle.

Work Border Stitch for 2.5"
Bind off neatly.
Work second sleeve.

Cardigan Finishing:
Front Neck:
Using smaller needle and RS facing, pick up 30 (32, 32) right front neck sts, 37(39, 39) back neck sts, 30 (32, 32) left front neck sts, 97[103, 103 sts]. Working back and forth, work border stitch for 6 rows. Bind off loosely in pattern.

Button Band: Left Front
With smaller needle and RS facing, pick up 99, (104, 106) sts along front edge. Work border stitch for 7 rows ending on wrong side. Bind off neatly.

Buttonhole Band: Right Front
With smaller needle and RS facing, pick up 99, (104, 106) sts along front edge. Work border stitch for 3 rows ending on wrong side row.
Buttonhole Row: Work 3(2, 3) sts in pattern, bind off 2sts, [work 11 (12, 12) sts , bind off 2] 7x, work to end.
On next row, cast on 2 sts over bound off sts.
Complete band as for left front.

Pullover Finishing:
Neck Trim:
With size 7 16" circular needle, pick up 104 (112, 120) sts around the neck. Join. Work in border stitch for 6 rounds. Bind off loosely.
Seam sides and sleeves.

Block and Shape.

Ellen's Socks

Size: Woman's Medium
Materials:
2 hanks Shelridge Farm Soft Touch Ultra (3-Ply Fingering Weight)
Color: Storm
Needles: 2.5 mm 5 dpns.
Tapestry needle.
Pin type marker.

Gauge: 8 sts/in, 10 rws/in worked in stockinette stitch.

Leg Pattern:

| Knit
— Purl

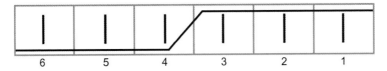

Right Cross Cable: Insert right needle point into the front of the 4th, 5th & 6th stitch on the left needle point. Slide stitches onto right needle point. Stitches 1, 2 & 3 will drop to back. Pick up dropped stitches with left needle point. Slip first three stitches from right needle to left needle. Knit 6 stitches.

Cable Chart

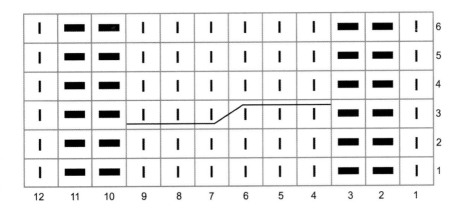

Cast On:
Cast on 72 sts loosely.
Division of Stitches: Please note stitches are divided in a manner not to divide any cable between needles. The beginning of the round is on the side of the sock on the 4 dpns rather than in the middle of the heel.

N1: 12 sts heel
N2: 24 sts heel
N3: 12 sts instep
N4: 24 sts instep

Join. Mark for beginning of round.
Cuff:
Round 1: K1, *p2, k2. Repeat from * end k1.
Work Round 1 12 times total.

Leg:
Work cable chart for 7" ending on round 5.
Round 6: K1, *p2, k2 tog. 3times (reducing the cable from 6 stitches to 3 stitches), p2, k2. Repeat from * end k1 (54 stitches).

Rearrange stitches in the following manner. Slip next 27 stitches onto one needle to work the heel flap. Divide the instep stitches as follows, 14 stitches on one needle, 13 on a second needle.

Heel Flap worked over 27 stitches:
The heel flap is worked in Slip 1, K 1 heel stitch with a garter stitch border.
Row 1: K3, *Slip 1 as to purl, k1. Repeat from star to last 3 sts, ending on slip 1. Knit 3.
Row 2: K3, purl to last 3 sts, K3.
Repeat Rows 1 and 2 until 28 rows are complete.

Turn Heel:
Note: Sl 1 = sl 1 purlwise
Rw 1: (RS) K15, ssk, k1. Turn.
Rw 2: Sl 1, p4, p2tog, p1. Turn.
Rw 3: Sl 1, k5, ssk, k1. Turn.
Rw 4: Sl 1, p6, p2tog, p1. Turn.
Rw 5: Sl 1, k7, ssk, k1. Turn.
Rw 6: Sl 1, p8, p2tog, p1. Turn.
Rw 7: Sl 1, k9, ssk, k1. Turn.
Rw 8: Sl 1, p10, p2tog, p1. Turn.
Rw 9: Sl 1, k11, ssk, k1. Turn.
Rw 10: Sl 1, p12, p2tog, p1. Turn.
Rw 11: Sl 1, k13, ssk. Turn.
Rw 12: Sl 1, p14, p2tog. Turn.

Heel Gusset:
Knit 8 stitches – N1. Using a second needle (N2), complete row and

Continuing with the same needle, pick up 14 sts along the left side of the heel.
Pick up and knit st from the row below the first instep st to prevent a hole.

Instep sts at rest on N3:14 sts, N4: 13 sts (27 sts total).

Work across instep in pattern as follows:
K1, p2, k3, p2, k2, p2, k3, p2, k2, p2, k3, p2, k1

With free needle, pick up a stitch from the row below the first heel st to prevent a hole.

Pick up 14 sts along the right side of the heel and k across sts on N1. K across N2. Place a marker. The marker represents the start of the instep. (N3, N4)

Shape Gusset:
Dec. Rnd
N3: (instep) Work sts in established pattern
N4: (instep) Work in pattern.
N1: (heel) K1, ssk knit to end of needle.
N2: (heel) K to the last 3 sts, k2tog, k1.

Next Rnd: Work even.

Repeat these two rnds until there are 54 sts remaining.

Foot:
Continue working in rounds until foot measures 7.9" or 2" from desired finished length. End at instep marker.

Shape Toe:
Instep pattern stops here. Knit all rounds.

Rnd 1:
N3: (instep) K1, ssk, knit to end of needle.
N4: (instep) Knit to 3 sts before end of needle, k2tog, k1.
N1: (heel) K1, ssk, knit to end of needle.
N2: (heel) Knit to 3 sts before end of needle, k2tog, k1.
Rnd 2: Work even.

Repeat these two rnds until 26 sts
remain. [14 rnds]
Work Rnd 1 only until 14 sts remain (7 heel sts, 7 instep sts).

Finishing:

Slip instep sts onto one needle.
Slip heel sts onto another needle.

Graft toe using Kitchener Stitch
Weave in ends on inside of sock.
Work second sock.

Buttery Autumn

Size: S, M, L
Finished Chest: 40,46, 50
Pattern is written for either cardigan as pictured, or pullover.

Materials:
6,7,7 skeins Black Water Abbey Yarn
Color: Butter
Yardage 220 yds per skein, worsted weight.
8 7/8" buttons.
Tapestry needle.
Markers.

Needles:
US 6 (4mm), US 8 (5mm)

Gauge: 4.5 sts per in/ 6 rws per in over a stockinette stitch swatch.

Stitches:
Seed Stitch:
All seed stitch rows: *K1, P1; repeat from * end K1

Chart Stitches:

Knit on right side, purl on wrong side.

Purl on right side, knit on wrong side.

4st right cross

Insert right needle point into the front of the 3rd & 4th stitch on the left
needle. Slide stitches onto right needle. Stitches 1 & 2 will drop to back.
Pick up dropped stitches with left needle point. Slip first three stitches
from right needle to left needle. Knit 4 stitches.

4st left cross

Insert right needle point into the back of the 3rd & 4th stitch on the left

needle. Slide stitches onto right needle. Stitches 1 & 2 will drop to front. Pick up dropped stitches with left needle point. Slip first three stitches from right needle to left needle. Knit 4 stitches.

Knit & purl left cross

Insert right needle point into the back of the 3rd & 4th stitch on the left needle. Slide stitches onto right needle. Stitches 1 & 2 will drop to front. Pick up dropped stitches with left needle point. Slip first three stitches from right needle to left needle. Purl2, K2.

Knit & purl right cross

Insert right needle point into the front of the 3rd & 4th stitch on the left needle. Slide stitches onto right needle. Stitches 1 & 2 will drop to back. Pick up dropped stitches with left needle point. Slip first three stitches from right needle to left needle. Knit 2,p2.

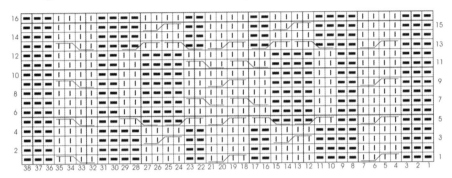

Back:

Note: Cardigan and pullover backs are worked the same.

With smaller needle, cast on: 89(103,111) sts. Work seed stitch as described above for 5 rws. On the 6th row, increase as follows increase 20 sts across the row as follows:

S: [Work 4, inc in next st, work 3 inc in next st] 5x. [Work 3, inc in next st] 10 x, end work 4. (109 sts)

M: [Work 4, inc in next st, work 3, inc in next st] 1x. [Work 4, inc in next st] 17 x. End Work 4; (123 sts)

L: [[Work 5, inc in next st, work 4, inc in next st] 6x. [Work 4, inc in next st] 8x. End work 5. (131 sts)

Change to larger needle. Set up row: Wrong side.

P 10,(16,18) place marker, [k3, p4,k4,p4,k2,p4,k2,p4,k4,p4,k3], place marker, p 11(15,19) place marker, repeat sequence between [], place marker end p 10(16,18).

Row 1: RS. K10,(16,18), work chart, k11,(15,19), work chart, end k10,(16,18). The pattern is established, 3 panels of stockinette stitch, 2 panels of cable stitch.

Repeat chart rows 1 – 16, 5x. End on a row 15.

On the next row, dec 20 sts as follow: P 10,(16,18) pass marker, [k3, p2tog,p2tog,k4,p2tog,p2tog,k2,p2tog,p2tog,k2,p2tog,p2tog,k4,p2tog,p2tog,k3], pass marker, p 11(15,19), pass marker, repeat seqence between [], pass marker, end p 10(16,18).
Next row: RS. Change to seed stitch and remove markers. Work in piece measures 9.5(9.5,11)" from the undearm markers (beg of seed stitch bodice).

Bind off all stitches; 30(35,39) shoulder sts, 29(33,33) back neck sts, 30(35,39) shoulder sts.

Pullover Front: Work same as back until piece measures 7(7.5,8)" from underarm marker (beg of seed stitch)
Neck Shaping:
On the next row, work to the center 18(20,20) stitches. Attach a second ball of yarn. Bind off center 18(20,20) sts. Dec 1 st each neck edge, every other row, 6(7,7) x. Continue working in seed stitch until front matches the back in length. Bind off across each shoulder.

Cardigan Fronts:
Make two, reversing shaping.
Cast on 45(51,55)sts. Work seed stitch border as for back.
On the last row, increase 10 sts as follows:
S:(Work 4, inc 1 in next st) 1 x, (Work 3, inc 1 in next st) 9 x, end work 4
M:(Work 4, inc 1 in next st, Work 3, inc 1 in next st) 3 x, (Work 4, inc 1 in next st) 4 x, end work 4
L; (Work 5, inc 1 in next st) 10x, end work 5.
Change to larger needles. Set up row.
p   8,(11,13), place maker [k3, p4,k4,p4,k2,p4,k2,p4,k4,p4,k3]place marker, p 9(12,14).
Work as for back and at the same time when seed stitch measures 7(7.5,8)" from the underarm marker (beg of seed stitch) begin neck shaping.
Bind off 9(10,10)sts at neck edge then Dec 1 st each neck edge, every other row, 6(7,7). Continue working in seed stitch until front matches the back in length. Bind off across each shoulder.

Seam Shoulders.

Sleeves:
Sleeve are worked in stockinette stitch to cuff.

Pick Up Sleeve Sts
At armhole edge, with larger needle, and RS facing, pick up 86 (86,100)sts between armhole markers.

Shape Sleeve

Dec 1 st on each side every 3(4,3) rws, 8(5,14)x then every 4(5,4) rws, 15(14,12)x. 40(48,48) sts.Continue in stockinette st until piece meas 15 (16,16)". On the last row, dec 1 st. 39(47,47) sts.

 Change to smaller needles and work seed stitch for 2.5". Bind off.

Seam sleeves.
Seam sides.

Neck Finishing:
Pullover: Using 16" circular needle in smaller size, pick up 80(94,94) sts around neck. Join. Work seed stitch for 6 rnds repeating rnds 1 & 2 three times.
Rnd 1:* K1, P1, repeat from * around.
Rnd 2: * P1, K1, repeat from * around.
Bind off.

Cardigan: Using smaller needle and RS facing, pick 81(95, 95) sts for neck band. Work seed stitch for 6 rws. Bind off.

Cardigan Bands:

Finishing Bands: Left Front
With smaller needles and RS facing, pick up 103 (103, 111) sts. Work in seed st border for 8 rws. Bind off.

Right Front
With smaller needles and RS facing, pick up 103 (103, 111) sts. Work in seed st border for 3 rws.
Row 4: Continue in seed sts, work buttonholes as follows: Work 6(6, 6)* bind off next st, work 12(12,13) repeat 7 times total, end bind off 1, work 5(5.6).
Row 5: Continue in seed stitch, cast on one stitch over bound off stitch. Complete as for left band.

Weave in ends.
Sew button in place.

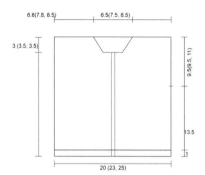

Cardigan body.

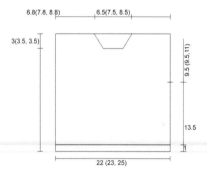

Pullover body.

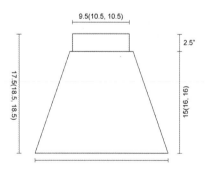

Sleeve.

44